P9-APN-120

ALCATRAZ

Text by
RICHARD DUNBAR

Edited by
KEN GLASER, JR. & KEVIN KENNY

Photos by
ANDREA PISTOLESI

BONECHI
SNC

SMITH NOVELTY COMPANY
San Francisco, CA 94103, U.S.A.
e-mail: snco@smithnovelty.com

© World Publisher - Firenze - Italia
© Casa Editrice Bonechi - Firenze - Italia
E-mail: info@bonechibooks.it
Internet: www.bonechi.com
On Instagram:
Follow us @bonechi_edizioni
Tag us #bonechibooks

Collective work. All rights reserved.
No part of this publication may be reproduced, stored,
or transmitted in any form or by any means, whether
electronic, chemical, or mechanical, by photocopying
or by any other system including radio, television,
or by any information storage and retrieval system,
without the express written permission of the publisher.

The cover and layout of this publication are the work
of Publishing House graphic artists and as such
they are protected by international copyright.

Printed in Italy.

The photographs are property of the Publishing House
Archives.

Other contributors:
Courtesy of the Golden Gate National Recreation Area: Don
Denevi Photographic Collection: page 8, page 13 (above), page
14 (above), page 15 (above and below), page 16 (above and
below), page 18, page 19 (above and below), page 20, page
26, page 29 (above and below), page 33 (above and below),
page 35, page 37 (below), page 38 (above and center), page 39
(below), page 41, page 42, page 43 (above and below), page 44
(above), page 45, page 46, page 49 (above and below), page 50
(above and below), page 51 (above and below), page 52, page
53, page 54, page 55 (above and below), page 56 (above left and
above right), page 57, page 58 (above and below), page 59, page
61. Tom Mulhern Photographic Collection: page 12 (above).
Charles Berta Photographic Collection: page 44 (below). Arnold
W. Peters Photographic Collection: page 47 (below).
Courtesy of The Bancroft Library, University of California at
Berkeley: page 10 (above, center, below), page 11 (above),
page 13 (below).

Courtesy of Ken Glaser Jr.: page 17, page 21, page 31 (below),
page 34 (above), page 40 (above), page 47 (above), page 62,
page 63, page 67 (below right), page 68, page 69 (above and
below), page 72 (above), page 80 (above), page 82, page 88,
page 89, page 90 (below), page 91 (above), page 92, page 93
(above and below), page 94 (below), page 95.
Courtesy of the Marilyn Blaisdell Collection: page 3, page 9
(below).
Courtesy of Mary Beth Barber: page 94 (above).
Courtesy of Asteron Productions: page 56 (below).

Special thanks to the staff at the
San Francisco Maritime National Historical Park.

The publisher apologizes in advance for any unintentional
omissions and would be pleased to insert appropriate
acknowledgements in any subsequent edition of this publication
if advised by copyright holders.

ISBN 978-88-8029-940-0

INTRODUCTION

Jutting out of San Francisco Bay, **Alcatraz** Island is a must see landmark in one of the worlds favorite tourist destinations. Why would nearly a million visitors a year take the short ferry ride from Fisherman's Wharf to this barren rock island known for its chilly winds and fog?

They are drawn by the infamous history, the mystery and suspense created by the many movies and books about Alcatraz and morbid curiosity to see the damp and cramped cells where the most notorious criminals in the United States were incarcerated.

The island played an important role in the formative years of the city of San Francisco and the state of California. Alcatraz was the sight of the **first lighthouse** built on the West Coast, and was also an important **military fort** protecting San Francisco Bay.

Alcatraz continues to be best known for its 29 years as America's **ultra maximum security** prison, but visitors should also become acquainted with the interesting early years of the island's heritage. The early buildings and history of Alcatraz are not as visible as the main cellblock, or as dramatic as the tales of the famous prisoners and the escape attempts, but they are just as compelling.

The following pages will take you on an historical and visual journey from the early years of the island to the present. The harsh elements of mother nature are visibly weathering the remaining structures on Alcatraz and at various times of the year wildflowers and flowering iceplant color the otherwise gray landscape. Whether you visit Alcatraz in the early morning or late afternoon, the vistas of San Francisco, the Golden Gate Bridge, the hills of Marin County and the East Bay are ever changing and always spectacular.

Alcatraz Federal Penitentiary as it appeared in the 1930s, with Angel Island in the background.

Above: Alcatraz Island today, looking south towards the skyline of San Francisco. The treacherous currents of San Francisco Bay made escape by swimming all but impossible.

Opposite page: San Francisco through the shattered windows of the Laundry Building.

Pages 6-7: Since becoming part of the Golden Gate National Recreation Area and opening to the public in 1973, Alcatraz has attracted nearly one million visitors annually.

The island received its name in 1775, when Spanish explorers charted San Francisco Bay. The rocky island was called **La Isla de los Alcatraces**, *after a species of cormorants found in Spain. There was no fresh water on the island and the only vegetation was some hardy grass that managed to grow out of the limestone. It was not until California became a part of the United States that Alcatraz began to change. In 1853, the U.S. Army decided to build an impregnable defensive fortress on Alcatraz to protect the city of San Francisco and the Bay. At the same time, work began on the first West Coast lighthouse. Large parts of the island were blasted away to make room for the fort and gun emplacements. Tons of soil were also brought over from Angel Island, which today supports the lush vegetation that grows on sections of Alcatraz.*

While the island's fire power was never tested, its security as a prison soon was. Starting in 1861, only two years after the island opened as a military fortress, Alcatraz began receiving **Civil War prisoners** *and for the next decades the island was both a fort and a military prison. By 1910 Alcatraz was only a military prison and work was under way on the present cellhouse and lighthouse. The U.S. Army pulled out of Alcatraz altogether in 1934, but the island did not remain vacant. In August of that year, Alcatraz became an ultra maximum-security Federal Penitentiary. A crime wave had been sweeping the country during the years of Prohibition and the Great Depression and the federal government was looking for a secure place to imprison notorious gangsters and recalcitrant prisoners serving time in other Federal Penitentiaries. Thus, Alcatraz became home to* **Al Capone, George "Machine Gun" Kelly** *and* **Robert Stroud,** *the* **"Birdman of Alcatraz."**

Alcatraz Federal Penitentiary, *too expensive to maintain and its physical infrastructure deteriorating was closed in 1963. No one knew what to do with the island until, after the* **Native American occupation** *of 1969-1971, it became part of the new* **Golden Gate National Recreation Area** *in 1972.*

Above: A painting of Alcatraz with its first buildings in the 1850s.

Opposite, above: The Isle of Pelicans as seen in 1856, looking across Meiggs Wharf from the foot of Powell Street.

Opposite, below: By the early 1910s, the new cell block and lighthouse had been built on Alcatraz. Mt. Tamalpais in Marin County is visible in this westward facing view.

A BRIEF HISTORY

If you had been standing on today's northern edge of San Francisco some 10,000 years ago, you could have reached Alcatraz by hiking across the broad valley that is now occupied by the waters of the San Francisco Bay. Upon climbing Alcatraz, then a hill in that valley, you would have had a bird's eye view of a great river between you and another hill, today's Angel Island. The river carried the waters of the Sierra Nevada through the Golden Gate and into the Pacific Ocean. With the end of the ice age, the oceans rose and the bay, along with the island of Alcatraz, was born.

This barren and inhospitable island, buffeted by chilling fog-laden winds, had no source of fresh water and the only vegetation was some hardy native grasses. Alcatraz was not suited for humans but was, however, a perfect habitat for sea birds.

The Native Americans were the first visitors to the island. They traveled to the island in reed canoes to gather eggs and perhaps fish from the rocky shores.

Spanish explorers were the first Europeans to see Alcatraz and in the summer of 1775 the *San Carlos*, under the command of **Juan Manuel de Ayala**, was the first European ship to sail into San Francisco Bay. **Jose Canizares** was in charge of charting and naming the new Spanish territories and to what he described as an arid island he gave the name *La Isla de los Alcatraces*, after the cormorants (not pelicans) that he found there in abundance. But neither the Spanish, nor, after them, the Mexicans, put the island to any use. Only in 1853, when California was part of the United States, did Alcatraz begin to be altered.

Above, opposite top: The island's strategic position near the entrance of San Francisco Bay led the U.S. military to build its most important West Coast defensive military fortress on Alcatraz.

FORT ALCATRAZ

The island's strategic position near the entry of San Francisco Bay made it a logical point for defense after the discovery of gold in California in 1848. San Francisco soon became the second most important port in the nation, and work on building the fortifications began in 1853 and accelerated in 1861 with the start of the **Civil War**. The original plans calling for the emplacement of 68 smoothbore cannons on the island saw the number expand to 155, including three 50,000 pound *Rodmans*, which were capable of firing 400 pound shots a distance of three miles.

Perhaps because its firepower was imposing, the fort never had to fire a shot in defense of the Bay, and its defenses had grown obsolete by the late 1800s. Alcatraz ceased to be a military fort in 1907. Although today there are few remnants of the original fortress structures (these include the casemate brick barracks near the wharf and the guardhouse and **sally port**), the blasting, carving and digging that was carried out to make **Fort Alcatraz** irrevocably altered the face and shape of the island.

The alley moat (bottom, right) was part of the old fort.

10

Above: In 1854, the first U.S. lighthouse on the West Coast was built on Alcatraz. The present lighthouse was built in 1909.

MILITARY PRISON

In 1861, only two years after the island opened as a military fortress, the Civil War broke out and Alcatraz began receiving its first prisoners. Thus the island's most infamous identity, that of a prison, began to take hold. Among the first prisoners were soldiers and officers who either supported the cause of the Confederate States or refused to take an oath of allegiance to the federal government.

In 1862, **President Abraham Lincoln** suspended the right of due process. This led to an influx of civilian detainees, many of them prominent Californians, who publicly or privately criticized the government or backed the South. The largest single influx of Civil War prisoners occurred when Lincoln was assassinated. In April 1865, prisoners were shipped to the island and spent two months performing hard labor.

After the war, Alcatraz continued serving as a military prison while structures were renovated and some new ones built, to accommodate men charged with desertion and felony offenses. The small prison population on the island fortress ballooned with the **Spanish American War** of 1898 and by 1900 about 450 men were detained there.

In 1906, Alcatraz hosted its first civilian inmates in several decades, when fires devastated San Francisco after the April 1906 earthquake. Their short stay was a harbinger of the island's future, as was the official designation in 1907 of Alcatraz as the **U.S. Disciplinary Barracks, Pacific Branch**. No longer a military fortification, the wind swept rock in the middle of San Francisco Bay hosted only military convicts, military guards and their families. The present cellhouse was added between 1909 and 1912 out of the need to build more secure detention facilities.

Ultimately, however, the island prison, which later became known as **"Uncle Sam's Devil's Island,"** was a controversy. The U.S. Army thought such a visible example of severe military discipline in the middle of a busy harbor shed bad light on the Army's reputation. Many civilians also felt uneasy about the presence of prisoners on Alcatraz. Critics complained of the harsh conditions under which the prisoners were forced to live. These denunciations, along with the cost of operating the prison, led the military to close the prison in 1934. Less then a month after the last military personnel left Alcatraz, the island's new and most famous phase, that of a Federal Penitentiary, began.

Above: Work on the present cellhouse began in 1909, after Alcatraz was designated solely as a military prison.

Below: Topsoil carried over from Angel Island made it possible to plant gardens on The Rock. Eventually, gardening became one of the favorite pastimes for the families living on the island.

Above: In 1934, Alcatraz became a maximum-security, minimum-privilege Federal Penitentiary.

Opposite, above: Alcatraz viewed from Fisherman's Wharf.

Opposite, below: A series of metal detectors, called "snitch boxes" or "stool pigeons," were set up in various points in the prison.

FEDERAL PENITENTIARY

As the U.S. military announced its intention to close the prison on Alcatraz, the Department of Justice stepped in with plans of its own. A crime wave sweeping the country during the years of **Prohibition** and the **Great Depression** prompted justice officials to look for a secure prison that could house some of the country's best known criminals as well as some of the Federal Penitentiary system's most hardened and incorrigible inmates. Alcatraz, with its still relatively new facilities, its isolated position and foreboding reputation could fit the bill.

Thus, when the first prisoners arrived from other Federal Penitentiaries in 1934, Alcatraz embarked on its 29 year history as a **maximum security penal institution of the federal government**, a legacy for which it is still best known today. In August of that year, 11 inmates joined 32 prisoners left behind by the military. Less than two weeks later in August, train carriages carrying 53 prisoners from Atlanta were put aboard a barge in Tiburon and transported to Alcatraz. Among those men was one of the penitentiary's best known inmates, **Al Capone**.

While the main structure of the prison remained unaltered, numerous modifications were made to render it more secure against escapes. Soft steel bars in the cells were replaced with tool proof bars. A new locking system which enabled cell doors to be opened individually was installed. Gun galleries overlooking the cellblocks and the dining hall were built, tear gas canisters were placed in the dining hall and cell blocks, a series of metal detectors were set up, and five guard towers were erected. In fact, of the 14 attempted escapes from The Rock, most were foiled immediately, and those men who were never accounted for were presumed victims of the Bay. By the early 1960s, Alcatraz's days as a prison were numbered. The deteriorating island prison was expensive to operate and continued to suffer from a poor public image. In March of 1963 the penitentiary closed. For the first time in 102 years, the fog swept island would no longer operate as a prison. In place of humans, nature would return once more and reclaim this small rocky island.

THE INDIAN OCCUPATION

After the closure of the Federal Penitentiary, the fate of the island remained uncertain. But while numerous proposals were being studied, Indian activist **Richard Oakes** and a group of 90 Native Americans and their sympathizers landed at the wharf on Alcatraz on November 20, 1969, beginning the occupation of the island that would last until the summer of 1971.

The group proposed converting Alcatraz into a center of culture and education for **Native Americans**. Although the federal government had no intention of negotiating the passage of the property to the Indians, the favorable public sentiment forestalled any action on the part of the government to remove the occupiers. Oakes departed in January 1970, following the accidental death of his daughter. By June 1, 1971, when fires gutted several structures on the neglected island, only a handful of occupiers remained. Ten days later, federal agents landed on the island and removed the last few Indians living on Alcatraz.

AS A NATIONAL PARK

Debate over the destiny of Alcatraz officially ended on October 12, 1972 when the **Golden Gate National Recreation Area** was formally established. Among its original 34,000 acres of urban and rural parklands were the 22 acres of Alcatraz. One year later, Alcatraz began receiving its first civilian visitors, who today number nearly one million annually.

Over the years, more of the island has gradually been opened to the public. Although the rubble of demolished buildings and the burnt out shells of others continue to make extensive parts of the island off limits to visitors, other obstacles and hazards have been removed. The area including the parade grounds, where the rubble from the former apartments that housed the guards and their families can be seen, has recently been opened to the public and a new walkway and promenade has been added to the southern end of the island. Future plans includes restoration of several historically significant buildings, such as the 1858 Guardhouse.

Opposite page: An occupation led by Native Americans brought changes to the island between 1969 and 1971.

Below: Alcatraz became part of the Golden Gate National Recreation Area in 1972.

Above: When Alcatraz became a Federal Penitentiary in 1934, numerous changes were made to ensure the prison would be escape-proof.

Opposite: Among the works carried out to make Alcatraz escape-proof was the construction of six guard towers. When all six towers were in operation, all parts of the island could be kept under surveillance.

FEDERAL PENITENTIARY

Alcatraz is best remembered for its 29 years as a tough and grim **maximum security Federal Penitentiary** that hosted some of America's best known and most notorious criminals.

In the depression and prohibition years of the early 1930s, the United States was being swept by an unprecedented crime wave. Gangsters in cities amassed fortunes and spread terror among rivals as they took control of the illicit and highly profitable liquor trade. In the American heartland, bands of criminals, like **Bonnie and Clyde** and the **Ma Barker Gang**, roamed the countryside robbing banks and post offices in small isolated rural towns. The U.S. government responded by establishing the **Federal Bureau of Investigation**. Slowly but surely, J. Edgar Hoover and his G-men started nabbing America's most wanted criminals.

As the U.S. military moved forward with its plans to abandon Alcatraz, the U.S. Department of Justice started looking for a maximum security prison

where it could keep high profile prisoners as well as those who proved to be the most recalcitrant and disruptive. The windswept rocky island situated in beautiful San Francisco Bay seemed to fulfill the government's requirements. The facilities were relatively new and the cold treacherous currents of the Bay would deter escape attempts. Its visible setting in a major urban area would provide a constant reminder to both criminals and the public that the FBI was enforcing the law of the land. The combination of "The Rock's" visibility, isolation and its reputation of being a grim harsh prison, created an aura of notoriety and mystery that the government was quite willing to promote.

In October 1933, the Department of Justice acquired the Island and following renovations officially opened the nation's first ultra-maximum security Federal Penitentiary on July 1, 1934. The first warden, **James A. Johnston**, personally supervised the upgrades that he hoped would make the prison escape-proof. He also hand picked

UNITED STATES
PENITENTIARY
ALCATRAZ ISLAND AREA 12 ACRES
1½ MILES TO TRANSPORT DOCK
ONLY GOVERNMENT BOATS PERMITTED
OTHERS MUST KEEP OFF 200 YARDS
NO ONE ALLOWED ASHORE
WITHOUT A PASS

Opposite: Tower duty was considered the worst assignment by correctional officers.

Next pages:
The cellhouse and recreation yard as they appear today.

his guards and personally conducted tours to mollify worried Bay Area officials, whose constituents were nervous about having America's most hardened criminals so close to their homes.

Several features made Alcatraz unique among U.S. prisons. The rules were extremely rigid. The only rights prisoners enjoyed were food, clothing, shelter and medical care. Anything else, such as visits, work and mail, were earned privileges which could be lost through misconduct. Socializing among prisoners was kept to a minimum. There was only one prisoner per cell and until 1937 there was even a rule of silence (it proved to be too oppressive and impossible to enforce). Convicts destined to serve time on Alcatraz were chosen from other Federal

Penitentiaries. Prisoners awaiting release were first sent elsewhere, as prison officials did not want the local press to have easy access to the ex-cons' stories about life on "The Rock."

In August 1934, Alcatraz began receiving its new tenants from other Federal Penitentiaries. Criminal legends such as **Al "Scarface" Capone**, **George "Machine Gun" Kelly**, **Robert "Birdman of Alcatraz" Stroud**, **Alvin "Creepy" Karpis**, **Floyd Hamilton** (the driver for Bonnie and Clyde), and **Arthur "Doc" Barker** (the last surviving son of the Ma Barker Gang) settled into their cells. America's most visible and yet, secretive prison began to evoke the images that remain rooted in public consciousness, even decades after it was vacated.

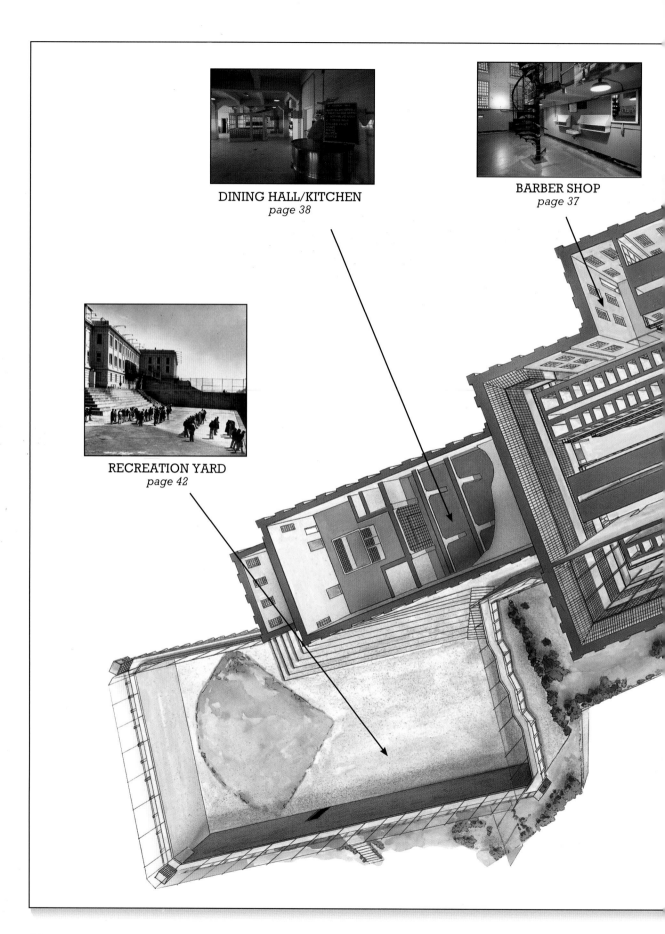

DINING HALL/KITCHEN
page 38

BARBER SHOP
page 37

RECREATION YARD
page 42

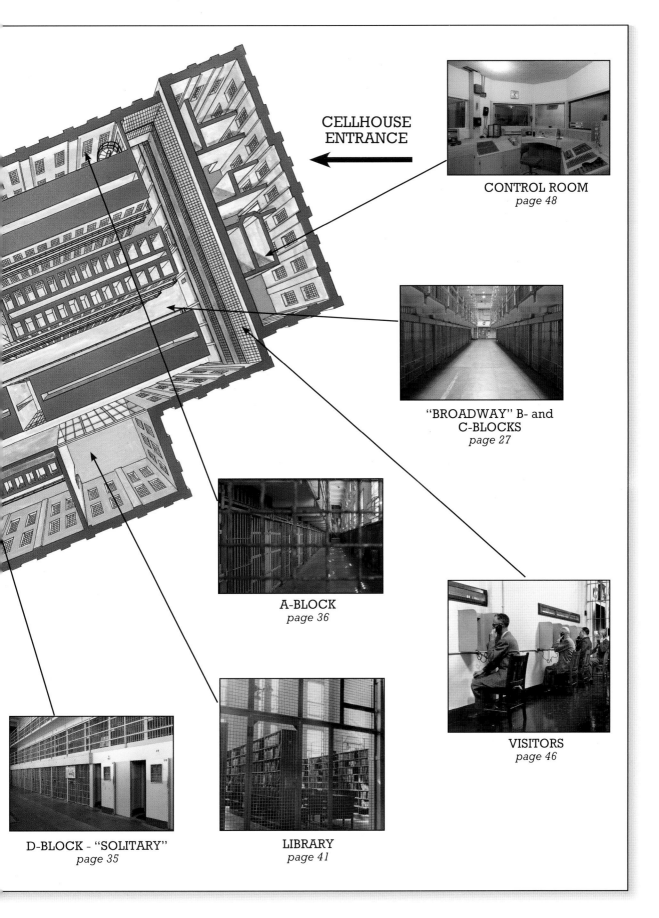

CELLHOUSE ENTRANCE

CONTROL ROOM
page 48

"BROADWAY" B- and C-BLOCKS
page 27

A-BLOCK
page 36

VISITORS
page 46

D-BLOCK - "SOLITARY"
page 35

LIBRARY
page 41

BROADWAY, B- AND C-BLOCKS

One of the features of Alcatraz that attracted Department of Justice officials in the early 1930s was the relatively modern cellhouse, which had been built by the U.S. Army between 1909 and 1912. The cellhouse was one of the largest reinforced concrete structures of its time. The four cellblocks: A, B, C, and D, contained 600 cells on three tiers. The cellblocks stood within the cellhouse, so that no cell adjoined with an outside wall. If a convict somehow managed to tunnel though his cell wall, he was still inside the main prison building.

When the first warden of the Federal Penitentiary, **James A. Johnston**, was asked to oversee the works that would make Alcatraz escape proof, he decided that the prisoners would be confined to B- and C-Blocks, since the prisoner population was not to exceed 300. Therefore, the cells in these two blocks underwent several modifications, while the cells in A-Block remained unaltered. Two of the most important improvements undertaken were the replacement of the softer flat iron bars (which could be more easily pried open) with thicker hardened steel bars and the installation of a new centralized cell locking system. This new system allowed any number of selected cells to be opened and locked simultaneously.

Opposite page: Guard Keith Dennison in the main cellblock in March 1963, the month Alcatraz Federal Penitentiary closed.

Below: A view down "Broadway" between B- and C-Blocks.

The main corridor dividing B- and C-Blocks was dubbed **"Broadway"** and the open area at the north end of the cellblock that led into the dining hall was called **"Times Square."** "Broadway," especially the ground floor, contained the least desirable cells. They were colder, had less privacy and were darker than the other cells. New inmates spent a month in quarantine in "Broadway." White and black prisoners were segregated up until the last years of the prison's operations.

Correctional officers who could be in direct contact with inmates were unarmed and carried no keys. The only armed guards were those who manned the watch towers and the two caged gun galleries, which had been built at the south and north ends of the cellblock in 1934. The officers on duty in the gun galleries kept watch over the cellblocks and the dining hall and stood ready to shoot if the situation demanded it. They also lowered keys to the guards on the ground when they were needed.

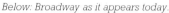

Top, left: A reconstructed cell showing what guards discovered during the famous escape attempt in 1962.

Below: Broadway as it appears today.

Life in the cells at Alcatraz around 1960.

Pages 30-32: Different perspectives of the cellblocks and cells on Alcatraz, as seen today.

Midway down **"Broadway,"** the two main cellblocks were interrupted. This area was called the **"cut-off"** and it permitted guards to pass between the cellblocks and cover the entire cellhouse more effectively. The **"utility corridor"** is a narrow passage bisecting the cellblocks over their entire length. The corridor served to bring plumbing, electricity and ventilation ducts into the cells. These passages provided a route out of the cellhouse in what was the most famous and ingenious, escape from Alcatraz. On June 11, 1962, three prisoners ended months of preparation by slipping through the ventilator holes in the back of their cells and into the utility corridor. From there, they gained access to the roof of the cellhouse,

from which they made it to the Bay. They were never seen or heard from again. It is presumed they drowned in the strong currents that were flowing through the Golden Gate and into the Pacific Ocean that night.

Six guards generally patrolled the main cellblocks during the hours in which prisoners were in their cells. Besides the frequent headcounts, random headcounts took place as well as random inspections of the cells and bars. Guards also oversaw the work of the orderlies, who kept the cellblocks spotless. Bars railings and windows were cleaned daily and the floors were kept shining by woolen blankets discarded by the U.S. military.

Above: Unidentified guards in the main cellblock of Alcatraz Federal Penitentiary around 1960.

Lower right: San Francisco Mayor Angelo Rossi, U.S. Attorney General Homer Cummings, Warden James A. Johnston and San Francisco Police Chief William Quinn touring Alcatraz in August, 1934.

Some of the 42 cells in D-Block, officially known as the Treatment Unit or Isolation. Inmates in isolation were allowed out of their cells only twice a week, once to bathe and once to go to the recreation yard.

SOLITARY CONFINEMENT

An inmate's life on "The Rock" was hard enough, of course, but it could get worse. Loss of privileges such as books from the library, access to the workshops or exercise yard, was but a first step in a progressive regimen of sanctions. The next stop was D-Block. What could get a prisoner sent there? At the very top of the list was an assault on a guard. Extreme physical violence may have been fairly rare but guards were frequently spat upon, pelted with food, urine or feces. Escape attempts would also land you in D-Block. Then there was a wide and loosely defined variety of offenses, grouped best under the heading of "bad attitude", such as cursing a guard, chronic boisterousness or refusing to carry out directions.

D-Block contained forty-two cells and there was an ascending scale of punishment severity, from Isolation to Solitary to the Strip Cell. Isolation consisted of thirty-six cells, which were identical to those of the regular cell blocks. The difference was that inmates in Isolation remained in the cells twenty-four hours a day. They took their meals there and were allowed one shower (fifteen minutes) per week and given one hour per week in the exercise yard. One of the ways a prisoner could be sent to Isolation was to be so disagreeable or unstable that he had to be kept apart from the general inmate population. This was the case with **Robert Stroud, "The Birdman of Alcatraz."** Although Isolation was meant

as the rung in the ladder of D-Block discipline, it also served as semi-permanent home for Stroud, who occupied Cell # 42 for several years before the kidney ailment known as Bright's Disease caused his transfer to the prison hospital. After Isolation there was Solitary or the Hole, as it was called. It consisted of five cells with only a toilet and sink, and a solid steel door which when shut (which was twenty-four hours a day, save for meals), left the inmate in complete darkness. Mattresses were issued each evening at bedtime then removed each morning. Prisoners typically would spend anywhere from three to nineteen days in Solitary. The mental and emotional toll could be very high and finding ways of passing the time could be critical. Former inmate Jim Quillan told of a game he played, he would flip a button into the air, disorient himself by turning around several times and then search for the button on his hands and knees. When he found the button he would repeat the process, again and again.

The very end of the line was the Strip Cell, there was only one. As with Solitary, the Strip Cell was completely dark. In addition, there was neither a toilet nor sink, only a hole in the floor and the cell itself was not the only thing stripped. Prisoners were frequently put in naked, usually as punishment for destruction of their clothes, mattresses, or blankets. Time in the Strip Cell was generally brief, usually two days.

Top: A-Block was used sparingly during the years that Alcatraz was a Federal Penitentiary.

A-BLOCK

A-Block never housed inmates while Alcatraz was a Federal Penitentiary and in fact was never modernized for this purpose. Therefore, with its flat strap-iron bars, key locks and spiral staircases, it is the only example of the original cellblocks that were built when the island was a military prison.

A-Block was used sparingly, but occasionally, troublemakers would be placed there, as would prisoners awaiting a hearing or a transfer. Starting in the late 1940s, prisoners were allowed to use the cells in A-Block to type documents, such as legal briefs for their lawyers. Some of the cells on this block also feature graffti left behind by some of the prisoners temporarily housed in this portion of the cellhouse.

BARBER SHOP

The small **barber shop** at the end of A-Block served only for the monthly haircuts that the inmates received. Shaving three times a week was obligatory for prisoners, a rule that was strictly enforced. But prisoners shaved in their cells after dinner.

Each prisoner was issued a shaving mug, shaving soap and a brush. The razor blades were handed out by the guards and prisoners had thirty minutes to shave and give back the razor. Those who couldn't account for their blades were sent to solitary confinement. Razor blades not only represented a deadly weapon that a prisoner could use against another inmate or a guard. They were also a danger to potentially suicidal men. Although a suicide attempt might likely not finish in death, it could be sufficient to get the prisoner transferred to another, less harsh, prison.

Spiral staircases leading to the barbershop. Many of the cellbock's spiral staircases were removed in 1934, when Alcatraz became a Federal Penitentiary (right).

Above: Inmates lining up for a meal in the last years of the Federal Penitentiary. The long tables and benches (below) were later replaced with smaller tables.

DINING HALL / KITCHEN

Food was one of the few essential rights accorded to prisoners and it was rumored that the food prepared on Alcatraz was among the best in the prison system. Perhaps because most other aspects of life on the "The Rock" were so difficult, it was thought that feeding the prisoners well could alleviate the overall hardship.

Twenty minutes were allowed for each of the day's three meals. Prisoners were allowed to take generous portions of food, but they were strictly prohibited from wasting anything. Those who did not finish what they had taken were not allowed their next meal.

The dining hall was considered one of the most dangerous places on the island. Meals were the only

21 MARCH 1963

ASSORTED DRY CEREALS
STEAMED WHOLE WHEAT
1 SCRAMBLED EGGS
2 FRESH MILK
STEWED FRUIT
TOAST
BREAD
BUTTER
COFFEE

Above: The menu, as it appeared on the prison's last day of operations.

Lower right: The switches to release gas from the canisters in the dining hall were never used.

time that prisoners were clustered together in close quarters, each of them with access to dinnerware which, of course, were potential weapons. Unarmed guards could do little to quell an uprising in the dining hall, so during meals, armed guards in the caged gun galleries above the hall kept close watch. The ceiling in the dining hall was also equipped with **tear gas canisters** in case trouble arose, but these were never used.

To help keep disturbances to a minimum, inmates were filed into the hall in a single line. When a table was filled everyone sat down in unison. In the first years of the penitentiary, an attempt was made to enforce a rule of silence throughout the prison, even in the dining hall. But this was revoked a few years after the prison opened. When inmates finished their

MESS HALL GAS RELEASE SWITCHES

CIRCUIT 1

CIRCUIT 2

CIRCUIT 3

EMERGENCY ALARM

meal, guards ensured all forks, knives and spoons were accounted for on each man's tray before the inmates were allowed to leave the hall.

Long tables and benches were replaced with four-man tables and chairs in later years, changing the appearance of the area from that of a mess hall to a cafeteria. On special occasions, such as holidays, musicians performed during meals.

The kitchen was staffed by prisoners, who were carefully inspected upon leaving the area at the end of their work shift. Knives, cleavers and other potentially lethal weapons were very carefully accounted for by guards.

SHOWER

Three times a week, inmates walked down a flight of stairs to the basement **shower room**. In addition to showering, the men received clean laundry, a roll of toilet paper and soap for their cells. It is said that the water was hot, about $100°$ F, so that the prisoners would not get used to cold water in case they ever thought about attempting an escape and confronting the chilly waters of San Francisco Bay. According to former prison officers, the shower room could be a particularly dangerous place. Stabbings and beatings among prisoners occasionally took place there.

Shower area as it appears today.

The books in the Alcatraz library, many of them donated from the U.S. Army, were one of the few diversions that inmates had when they were locked in their cells.

LIBRARY

The **library** was located in a room at the end of D-Block. The Federal Penitentiary inherited the army's stock of library books and over the years the collection grew to some 15,000 volumes. Since inmates were locked in their cells every evening from 5:30 onwards, reading was one of the few diversions available to them until the lights were shut offf at 9:30 p.m. Most prisoners preferred fiction, although law books were also popular for obvious reasons.

Each inmate had a **library card** and kept a catalogue of the library books in his cell. To order a book, a prisoner would fill out the request slip attached to his library card and drop it in a box at the entrance of the dining hall as he filed in for breakfast.

A library orderly would bring the requested book to the inmate's cell during the day. Inmates were allowed to keep three books in their cells at any one time, in addition to a Bible, dictionary and up to twelve text books. Library books that were not returned on their due date could cost the prisoner a temporary loss of their library privileges. Books did not contain any sex, violence or crime. The library also subscribed to several magazines. Prisoners were allowed to pay for subscriptions to selected magazines, which were checked by the prison censors when they arrived. Usually, after they had finished reading the magazine, inmates would circulate it to their friends among the prison population.

THE LIFE OF AN AVERAGE PRISONER

RECREATION YARD

In the years that Alcatraz was a Federal Penitentiary, there was much debate over the extent to which the conditions on "The Rock" were brutal, harsh and cruel. Designated to house the federal system's most difficult and most notorious inmates, Alcatraz was certainly not a holiday camp. Yet, it is thought that conditions there were not worse than in other prisons and in some aspects, such as the food, it was better. Apart from the climate, it seems that the biggest enemy that prisoners had to face day in and day out was boredom. Major diversions were jobs and the time spent in the **recreation yard**, as well as occasional movies, reading and in later years, radio. These were all privileges reserved for prisoners in good standing.

On weekends and holidays, the general inmate population could spend up to six hours in the recreation yard. Prisoners in Isolation were allowed to go to the yard alone or in small groups on a weekday and kitchen workers, who had seven day shifts, also could get exercise in the yard on weekdays. The favorite activities were card games (no gambling was permitted), dominoes, backgammon, chess, softball and shuffleboard. The overall favorite game was handball, for which two courts were provided. Prisoners could buy their own balls and gloves.

Since the recreation yard was the one place in the prison were inmates were allowed to spend long

Below: Inmates lining up for work details in the recreation yard in the 1950s.

and relatively unregimented time together, it was one of the most dangerous areas of the prison. Most of the assaults among prisoners occurred there, especially stabbings. Correctional officers, as elsewhere in the prison when they were in contact with the convicts, were unarmed. Armed guards kept an eye on the yard from catwalks that were perched along its perimeter. Typically, an assault on a prisoner would occur swiftly. Guards might notice a sudden commotion from a section of the yard. By the time guards arrived, they would find the injured man and other inmates who professed to have seen nothing. A code of silence was strictly enforced among the inmates.

Above: A guard at the top of the concrete steps in the recreation yard.

Below: Inmates enjoying the sun in the recreation yard.

Above: An armed guard stationed above the recreation yard. Any guard within reach of an inmate was unarmed.

Below: An inmate at work welding a submarine buoy.

Work was another way for prisoners to fight off the boredom of their incarceration. From 1942, it could also be a source, of income. But even without pay, work was a privilege and the only way for prisoners to avoid spending almost all of their time locked in their cells. The main industry on the island was the **laundry**, which served several military bases in the vicinity.

After breakfast, prisoners were marched to the recreation yard where they were lined up and given their work assignments. Most of the work took place in the industries buildings below the recreation yard. Walking to work was the furthest most inmates ventured past the concrete walls of the prison and the closest they could get to enjoying the open air and views of the Bay and San Francisco.

DAILY LIFE HOUR BY HOUR

The life of the prisoners was a highly regimented routine that varied little from day to day. The routine changed to a small extent over the years, becoming only slightly more lenient in later years. With the exception of those assigned to kitchen duty, prisoners worked five days a week. Movies were shown on some weekends and holidays.

6:30 a.m.	Morning gong. Prisoners get up, get dressed, make their bed, clean their cells.
6:50 a.m.	Second morning gong. Prisoners face their cell door for stand-up count. If count is accurate, cell doors are opened.
6:55 a.m.	Prisoners form a line and march single-file into dining hall.
7:00 a.m.	Breakfast. When prisoners finish breakfast, they place utensils on their trays and wait seated for guards to inspect the trays.
7:20 a.m.	End of breakfast. Prisoners working in industries march through door at the rear of the cellhouse and into recreation yard. Prisoners working in the cellhouse or those not working proceed to work positions or their cells.
7:25 a.m.	Guards and the prisoners assigned to their work details pass through a steel door in the recreation yard wall, detail by detail. Prisoners proceed down a flight of stairs, through a metal detector, and to their assigned shops.
7:30 a.m.	Inmates halt in front of their respective shop door for head-count by foreman, then proceed into shop and to work.
9:30 a.m.	Rest period. Inmates may smoke in designated areas.
9:38 a.m.	Whistle announces end of rest period. Head-count taken.
11:30 a.m.	Works stops. Prisoners assemble in front of shops for head-count. Prisoners pass through metal detector and proceed through rear door of recreation yard.
11:35 a.m.	Dining hall line forms in recreation yard. Prisoners proceed in single-file through cellhouse door and into dining hall for lunch.
11:40 a.m.	Lunch routine same as for breakfast, except that prisoners return to cells instead of work details.
12:00 p.m.	Prisoners return to cells and are locked up. Noon count is made.
12:20 p.m.	Prisoners working in shop details proceed to recreation yard, and follow same procedure as for morning details.
2:30 p.m.	Rest period. Same procedure and count as in morning.
4:15 p.m.	End of work. Prisoners are counted and follow same routine in proceeding to dining hall as in morning.
4:25 p.m.	Prisoners enter dining hall for dinner.
4:45 p.m.	End of dinner routine same as for other meals. Prisoners proceed to cells for final lock-up and count.
9:30 p.m.	Lights out.

Between the final lock-up and the switching off of the lights, two standing counts of the prisoners were taken. Two other cell counts were taken during the night.

VISITORS

Receiving **visitors** was a privilege that prisoners could take advantage of only once a month for a maximum of about 90 minutes. Visits were also limited to blood relatives and wives. A relative wishing to visit Alcatraz mailed a written request. Approved visitors would receive a letter instructing them to report to Pier 4 at **Fort Mason** in San Francisco at a given date and time. Once on Alcatraz, the visitor was driven to the main entrance of the cellhouse where he or she would pass through a metal detector before proceeding to one of the five visitor's stations. Prisoners and visitors spoke through telephones and were separated by five-inch bullet-proof glass windows. Prisoners were forbidden to discuss the prison or other inmates, at the risk of having the visit ended by the monitoring officer.

Visitors traveling from a long distance sometimes came at the end of the month so they could make a second visit in the first days of the following month. One famous visit apparently concerned **Al Capone's mother**. After setting off the metal detector several times, Mrs. Capone was finally stripped down to her garters, whose metal clips had been tripping off the alarm. She was said to be so flustered and angered by the event that she never returned to Alcatraz to visit her son.

LIFE IN A CELL

As the federal government's ultra-maximum security penitentiary, Alcatraz differed from other federal prisons in two important aspects. There was only one prisoner per cell, which measured five by nine feet (about 1.5 by 2.75 meters) and prisoners were locked in their cells from the time they returned from dinner, about 5 p.m., until they went to breakfast the next morning. In other prisons, cells were opened during the evening, allowing prisoners to visit.

Below: Inmates were allowed to have a 90 minute telephone visit with a member of their immediate family once a month.

This isolation and monotony made life particularly difficult for inmates on Alcatraz. In the early years, a silence rule was enforced. Despite this, prisoners invented ingenious ways to visit with inmates in neighboring cells. For example, they improvised checker boards, drawn with soap on the wall and silently communicated their moves with their neighbor. As the years passed, rules became more lax. The rule of silence was dropped, and inmates were allowed to keep checker boards or chess boards and play with neighbors (with each still locked in his cell). Some musical instruments were permitted and radio jacks were installed in the 1950s.

Top: A typical cell as seen today

Below: Prisoners sewing gloves in New Industries Building.

GUARD AND FAMILY LIFE ON THE ISLAND

In addition to its inmate population, Alcatraz was home to many of the men who worked there and to their families. Throughout the 29 years Alcatraz was a federal prison, women were never considered for positions as correctional officers. Working, and particularly living and growing up on "The Rock," was a unique experience. Living in the midst of one of the world's busiest and most beautiful harbors and next to some of the country's most notorious criminals, were as many as **60 families**. Most families considered Alcatraz a safe place to live, despite their proximity to the inmates. There was no city traffic, no city crime and contact between the residents and inmates was rare and usually only visual. The rocky cliffs above the Bay worried apprehensive parents more than possible dangerous encounters with a hardened criminal.

Most of the families were those of the correctional officers or guards, who usually numbered between 100 and 110. A minority of the officers were bachelors or lived on the mainland. Most guards were married and had families, which frequently grew during their stint on the island. Most of the children and wives who lived on the island fondly recall their experience, despite the fact that they lived on a wind swept island in poorly built apartments. The only playground was the two-acre concrete military parade grounds. It was a close-knit community and the children who commuted by boat daily to San Francisco to attend school were regarded by their peers with a certain sense of envy. Alcatraz was, after all, an enigmatic and mysterious place, which most people could only observe from afar. Much of the community life was centered in the social hall, the scene of parties, **dances**, **dinners** and a two-lane **bowling alley**. Boats between the island and San Francisco were frequent, as often as 22 times per day in the last years of the prison.

The days of the **correctional officers** nearly matched those of the prisoners in terms of the strict and repetitious routine. Officers carried out at least twelve official headcounts every day, as well as many more random counts. The dynamics of all the

The control room (below and next page) was the nerve center of the prison. All of the numerous headcounts taken every day and night were reported to the officer on duty in the control room.

personal relationships within the prison among inmates and guards could be strained and stressful. Officers had to be both fair and tough with the prisoners. Even an attempt at leniency, such as turning a blind eye to an infraction, would be perceived by the inmates as a weakness that would then probably be exploited to the greatest possible extent. At the same time, it was not to the advantage of the guards to earn the deep animosity of prisoners. Punishment, whether corporal or causing an inmate to lose privileges, should be commensurate with the offense committed. This seemed to be the fine line that correctional officers had to tread, in order to gain the respect and not the hatred, of most inmates. There are even stories of

Top: Guards in the cellblock did not carry keys, which were kept in the control room and by the guards in the gun galleries.

Bottom: Guards on Alcatraz, May 1946.

*Above: Attorney General Homer Cummings and
Warden James A. Johnston inspecting guards at the opening
of Alcatraz Federal Penitentiary in August, 1934.*

*Bottom: Inmates escorted out of Alcatraz in March, 1963,
when the prison closed.*

prisoners protecting guards from other prisoners
and of retired guards befriending released cons.

In the years that Alcatraz was a Federal Penitentiary,
three officers were killed by inmates as the result
of attempted escapes. Indeed, there were a few
inmates who were desperate enough to attempt an
escape and would not have hesitated to kill anyone
who stood in their way. Most assaults against the
guards occurred when prisoners were removed
from their cells by force to be placed in Isolation.
These inmates knew they had little to lose at that
point and looked at their physical resistance as a
question of pride.

Above: A portrait of wardens, correctional officers and staff at Alcatraz.

FAMOUS FACTS AND FIGURES

WARDENS

In its 29 years of history as a Federal Penitentiary, Alcatraz had four wardens, the top official was appointed by the Federal Bureau of Prisons. The island's first warden, **James A. Johnston**, was instrumental in directing the transition of the facility from a military prison to the country's top maximum security penitentiary.

Johnston, a retired California state prison official had become a lawyer and taken up a career in banking when he was called to become the first warden of Alcatraz. The former warden of **Folsom** and **San Quentin** prisons in California, Johnston, nicknamed "Saltwater" was an early reformer of the prison system. At Folsom, the work and rehabilitation

programs he instituted were considered radical. They were also successful and remained in place for many decades. At Alcatraz, however, his mandate was not to innovate. As the end of the line for the nation's most notorious and recalcitrant criminals, Alcatraz offered no rehabilitation and few privileges to inmates. Johnston was known for trying to enforce a rule of silence, which, however, was lifted after a few years.

The first warden personally supervised numerous changes to the prison that were meant to make it escape proof. Among these were the round hardened steel bars on the cell doors, new cell locking systems, gun galleries, metal detectors and the construction of guard towers. Johnston also hand-picked all the correctional officers who came to work at Alcatraz. When Bay Area politicians were wary of the idea of placing America's most wanted criminals in their midst, Johnson invited them to Alcatraz to assure them no prisoner would ever escape from there.

Warden Johnston was considered strict but fair by both the inmates and the officers. His successor, **Edwin Swope**, became warden in 1948 and remained there until 1955. Although he liberalized some of the institution's harsh rules, Warden Swope was unpopular both among his officers and the inmates. Many considered him condescending and faulted him for creating a high level of mistrust and tension among the guards.

The third warden of Alcatraz was **Paul J. Madigan**, who perhaps of all the wardens possessed the best requisites to run the country's top maximum security prison. Madigan had worked his way up through the system, serving at Alcatraz three times before being appointed warden. In the late 1930s, Madigan was the captain of the guards until he was

transferred. He returned in 1949 as Swope's Associate Warden. As Warden, Madigan was known by guards and prisoners as "promising Paul" due to his tendency to agree with whatever point of view was being presented to him at a given moment. Although he could not fulfill everyone's request, Madigan was known for continuing to liberalize many of the prison's harsh policies. Towards the end of Madigan's six year tenure, it started to become apparent the federal government was preparing to close its expensive and deteriorating escape proof prison. When Madigan was transferred in 1961, most thought that his replacement, **Olin Blackwell** had been brought in to oversee the prison's closure. In his 18 months as warden, Blackwell continued his predecessors' liberalization policies, to the point that some older hard nosed guards grew to mistrust him. The famous 1962 **"Escape from Alcatraz"** occurred during Blackwell's appointment and some held him indirectly responsible for creating the conditions that made the mysterious and spectacular escape possible. It is more likely, however, that the crumbling structure and cutbacks in federal funding were the major culprits.

James A. Johnston holds a press conference in May, 1946, when the "blast out" occurred.

Above: New prisoners, including Al Capone, arrived in train from Atlanta in the prison's first weeks of operation in August, 1934.

Clarence Carnes (left) participated in the 1946 "blast out," the bloodiest escape attempt in Alcatraz Federal Penitentiary.

Miran Thompson, Sam Shockley and Carnes were tried for their role in the "blast out" from Alcatraz. Thompson and Shockley were later executed at San Quentin (opposite, below).

PRISONERS

The names of some of men who served time on Alcatraz read from the annals of America's romanticized gangster era of the 1930s: **Al Capone, "Machine Gun" Kelly, Alvin "Creepy" Karpis, Floyd Hamilton,** the driver for Bonnie and Clyde, **Doc Barker,** one of Ma Barker's sons, and Roy Gardner, the last of the great train robbers. Another of "The Rock's" famous guests was **Robert Stroud,** immortalized as the **"Birdman of Alcatraz."** The general prison population tended to hold anyone who had become the **FBI 's Public Enemy # 1** with awe and respect.

Al "Scarface" Capone was one of the best known prisoners ever to serve time in an American jail. After arriving in Chicago from Brooklyn as a 20 year old in 1919, a year before Prohibition was instituted, Capone rose swiftly to head the most powerful underworld faction of the city and probably the country. While some held him responsible for ruthlessly murdering countless rivals, others regarded him as a sort of modern day Robin Hood and a generous benefactor of charities. Capone's world began to crumble when he was sentenced to ten years in prison for income tax evasion. Until Alcatraz opened in 1934, Capone served

time in Atlanta, where some joked that he had more authority than the warden. Capone was among the first prisoners transferred to Alcatraz in August 1934. On "The Rock" the harsh realities of being an inmate finally caught up with the gangster. In his five years on Alcatraz, Capone began showing signs of the advanced stages of syphilis. He also got less respect from inmates than he was accustomed to, even suffering a stabbing attempt. Because of his deteriorating physical state, Capone was transferred to another prison medical facility before the end of his prison term.

Robert "Birdman" Stroud arrived on Alcatraz in 1942 after already spending the previous 33 years in prison for having murdered a bartender in Alaska and a prison guard. Given the death penalty, Stroud later had his sentence commuted to life imprisonment in Isolation by **President Woodrow Wilson.** At Leavenworth Penitentiary in Kansas, Stroud began keeping and studying birds, which eventually led to the publication of two important books on bird diseases. On Alcatraz, Stroud was not permitted to have birds, and he spent most of his 17 years on the

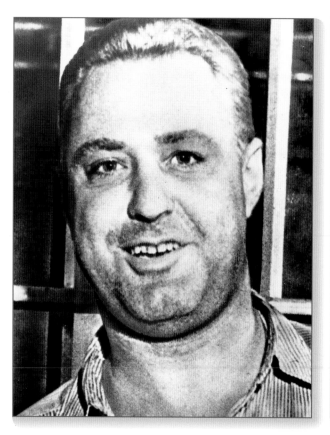

George "Machine Gun" Kelly (above left), Robert Stroud, the "Birdman of Alcatraz" (above right) and Al "Scarface" Capone (below, left) were among the best known inmates to spend time on Alcatraz.

Harmon Waley being escorted to Alcatraz in April, 1934 (next page, left).

The last prisoners leaving Alcatraz when it closed in March, 1963 (next page, right).

George Kelly and his wife Kathryn, being sentenced for kidnapping in an Oklahoma City court in October, 1933 (next page, below).

island either in isolation or in the prison hospital. Stroud was immortalized in the movie that was made while he was still living. While undoubtedly every bit the genius that he was portrayed to be in the film, Stroud was a difficult and violent man who had to be separated from the general inmate population.

The crime wave that swept the country in the 1920s and 1930s, fed first by Prohibition and then by the Great Depression, was characterized by gang activity controlling liquor trade in the cities and bands of armed robbers in the rural areas, particularly in the midwest. **George "Machine Gun" Kelly**, bank robber and kidnapper, belonged to the latter category, Kelly was finally apprehended by the FBI and sent to Alcatraz in 1934 and remained there until 1951, when he was sent to Leavenworth after suffering a mild heart attack. Kelly, who came from a wealthy family and was college educated, was remembered as being a soft spoken affable man. Among his jobs at Alcatraz, serving as the altar boy for the Catholic services and running the movie projector.

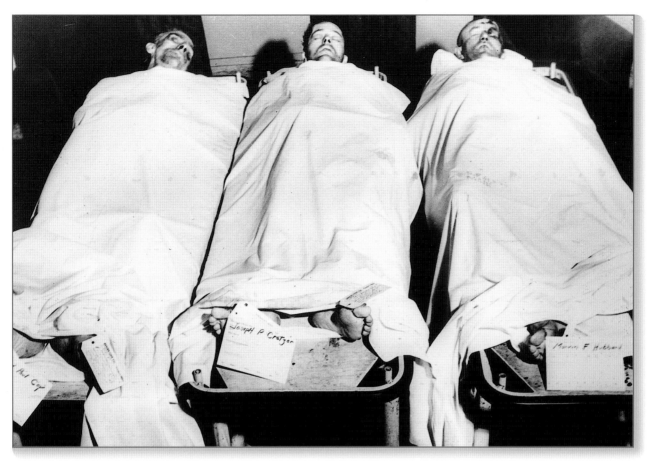

Opposite, above: This photo was taken during the "Battle of Alcatraz" in May of 1946.

Opposite, below: Aerial photos of Alcatraz showing the escape route followed by Anglin brothers and Frank Lee Morris in their famous 1962 disappearance. Although they were presumed drowned, none of the three men were ever found.

Above: Morgue shot of Bernard Coy, Joseph Cretzer and Marvin Hubbard after the unsuccessful breakout attempt in May of 1946.

ESCAPES

Alcatraz was highly touted as being escape proof, but whether that was true may be known only by those five men who managed to flee the island, never to be heard from or seen again. Between 1936 and 1962, 36 men broke out of Alcatraz or tried to, in **14 different attempts**. Of them, seven were shot and killed, one was found drowned in the Bay, five went unaccounted for and the remaining 23 were captured alive. Three guards were also killed in the escape attempts. The two most famous incidents were the 1946 **"Blast Out"** and 1962 **"Escape from Alcatraz."**

The **Blast Out**, also known as the **"Alcatraz Riot"** and the **"Battle of Alcatraz,"** began after lunch on May 2, 1946. Six inmates were involved in the break out, **Joseph Cretzer, Bernard Coy, Marvin Hubbard, Miran Thompson, Sam Shockley** and **Clarence Carnes**. The group's plan was carefully orchestrated, but went awry after they failed to procure the key that would have allowed them to open the door between the cellhouse and the recreation yard. The prisoners struck at a moment when only one unarmed guard was patrolling the cellhouse floor and one armed guard was positioned in the gun gallery. The two guards were overpowered by Coy and Hubbard, who armed themselves and opened the cells of the of B- and C-Blocks, allowing Carnes, Thompson and Cretzer to join them. Shockley was then liberated from his cell in Isolation. With their plans to leave the cellhouse foiled, the inmates began taking guards hostage. In all, nine guards were placed in cells 402 and 403, and eventually shot at by Cretzer. One of them, Officer **William Miller**, died, and several others were seriously wounded. In the meantime, guards, armed only with gas billies, began storming the cellhouse in the attempt to free the hostages, but had to withdraw as they drew fire from Coy, Cretzer and Hubbard. Another guard, **Officer Stites**, was killed (perhaps by friendly fire) as he stormed the cellhouse. The siege continued over the next two days, with the involvement of the U.S. Marines and Coast Guard. Eventually, the hostages were freed and it was ascertained that Hubbard, Coy and Cretzer had retreated to a utility corridor in C-Block. After firing machine gun volleys into the passageway and receiving no response, officers entered the corridor and found the lifeless bodies of the three inmates. The other inmates who had been involved, Carnes, Thompson and Shockley, were subsequently tried for the murder of Miller. Thompson and Shockley were sentenced to death in **San Quentin**'s gas chamber, while Carnes had another 99 years tagged onto his life sentence. In all, the Battle of Alcatraz had cost the lives of two officers and three inmates, with another fifteen officers wounded.

The **"Escape from Alcatraz"** occurred on June 11, 1962 and the three men involved, brothers **Clarence** and **John Anglin** and **Frank Lee Morris**, were never found. The escape involved months of meticulous planning, and was aided by the prison's deteriorating state and insufficient security due in large to cutbacks in funding. A fourth inmate, **Allen West**, was credited with devising the scheme. But

on the evening of the escape, he was unable to break out of his cell. The men spent months chipping at the crumbling air vents below the sinks in their cells. When they were finally able to pass through the vents, they climbed to the top of the cellblock each night, where they constructed life rafts out of raincoats. They had also constructed dummy heads from soap and concrete powder and hair collected from the barber shop. The heads were life like enough to fool guards as they made their rounds several times each night to count the prisoners while they slept. Finally, in the early morning of June 11, the men left the cells for the last time. Their absence was discovered in the morning, when officers reported that they could not wake up the three men. As a guard tapped the head of one of the prisoners, it rolled to the floor. No trace was ever found of the Anglin brothers and Morris and it was presumed they had drowned in the strong currents and cold waters of the Bay. This most ingenious of escapes from Alcatraz, help by a series of coincidences and oversights, was also made famous in the movie **"Escape from Alcatraz."**

The reconstruction of the cells where the famous
"Escape from Alcatraz began in 1962.

JOHN ANGLIN

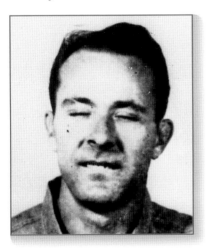

CLARENCE ANGLIN

FRANK LEE MORRIS

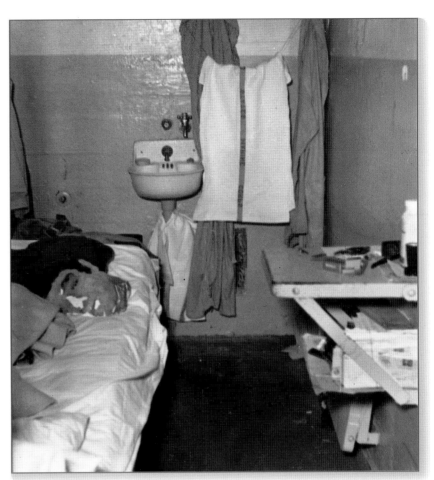

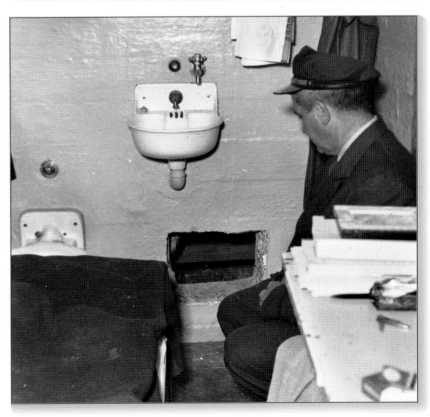

John Anglin's cell and dummy head (above). Senior Officer Waldron pointing out the enlarged air vent in the cell of Frank Lee Morris (right).

THE ISLAND TODAY

Today, Alcatraz is no less a wind swept, forlorn place as when it held some of the country's best known and most feared criminals. Although the prisoners have long abandoned the island, "The Rock" continues to hold a special place in the imagination of the public.

Since becoming part of the National Park System's **Golden Gate National Recreation Area** in 1972, Alcatraz has become one of the Bay Area's most popular destinations. Ferry boats carry nearly one million visitors to Alcatraz each year. Once on the island, visitors are free to walk around designated areas, join a guided tour led by **Park Rangers**, take a self-guided, audio-cassette tour of the cellhouse, visit the bookstore within the old military barracks, browse exhibits and watch a short informative documentary on the history of the island.

Access to many sections of the island is limited due to hazardous conditions caused by demolished and deteriorating structures. The **National Park System**, with the help of the non-profit **Golden Gate National Park Association**, is slowly opening more of the island to visitors, who are rewarded with spectacular views of **San Francisco Bay**, the city of **San Francisco** and the **Golden Gate Bridge**.

The island sits directly in the path of the fog bearing, chilly westerly winds that blow through the Golden Gate, particularly during summer afternoons. Coming prepared for a visit to Alcatraz means carrying a sweater or a jacket. Also bring comfortable walking shoes, as many paths are steep. Visitors can spend the entire day on the island, but must return with the last ferry to San Francisco (the schedule varies according to season). Although the ferry service is frequent, tickets sell out quickly, especially in the summer. Therefore, it is a good idea to purchase tickets in advance.

Top, below: Once inaccessible to local residents, Alcatraz has become one of the top attractions in the Bay Area.

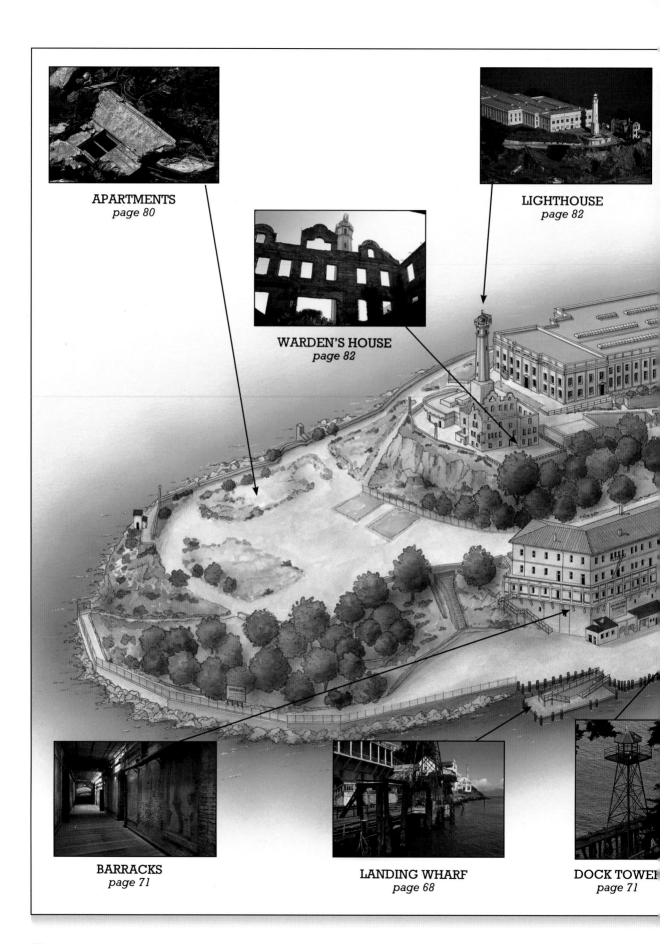

APARTMENTS
page 80

WARDEN'S HOUSE
page 82

LIGHTHOUSE
page 82

BARRACKS
page 71

LANDING WHARF
page 68

DOCK TOWE
page 71

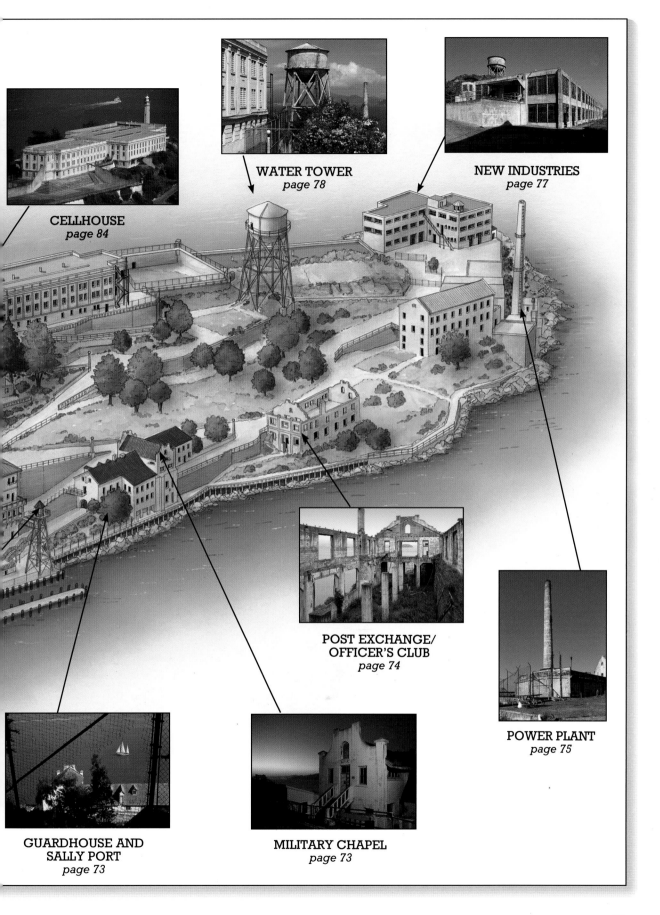

CELLHOUSE
page 84

WATER TOWER
page 78

NEW INDUSTRIES
page 77

POST EXCHANGE/
OFFICER'S CLUB
page 74

POWER PLANT
page 75

GUARDHOUSE AND
SALLY PORT
page 73

MILITARY CHAPEL
page 73

65

WARNING

PERSONS PROCURING OR
CONCEALING ESCAPE OF
PRISONERS ARE SUBJECT
TO PROSECUTION

LANDING WHARF

At the end of the short ferry ride from San Francisco, visitors disembark at the only landing wharf that Alcatraz Island has known. Built in 1854 at the island's only safe boat landing, the wharf was the starting point for many of the first structures built on Alcatraz: the barracks, the sally port and the first prison.

Inmates arriving to serve time on "The Rock" had their first direct contact with the island just as hundreds of thousands of tourists have now.

Today, the wharf area is the starting point for a visit to Alcatraz. Visitors are greeted by Park Rangers, who provide a short introduction about the island and give information on special activities of the day. Ranger led walks around Alcatraz, focus on topics such as military history, natural history, escapes, famous prisoners and the Native American occupation. Eating and smoking on the island are only permitted on the landing wharf, which is about a five minute walk from the cellhouse atop the island.

Pages 66 and 67: Aerial view of Alcatraz, with Industries Building in the foreground.

Visitors disembarking at the landing wharf after short ferry ride from San Francisco (below and next page). Since the island was first inhabited in 1853, the wharf has been the only docking point on the island.

DOCK TOWER

The **dock tower**, which rises above the landing wharf, is the only free standing guard tower left on Alcatraz. It was also one of the tallest guard towers in the United States. When Alcatraz became a maximum security Federal Penitentiary, six guard towers were constructed so that all parts of the island were under constant armed surveillance. In addition to the dock tower, there were guard towers on the west side of the recreation yard, at the northwest end of the island, at the powerhouse, on the roof of the cellhouse and on the roof of the model industries building.

Because of the cold and boredom, duty on the guard towers was one of the least favorite assignments of the officers. It was often reserved for guards who were young or under disciplinary action. When a boat arrived at the wharf, the officer in the dock tower would lower a cable to which the pilot of the boat would attach the keys. The keys were kept in the dock tower until the boat was ready to leave the island.

BARRACKS

The **barracks**, which today houses the bookstore, exhibit hall and theater is one of the oldest buildings on Alcatraz. The ground floor was built between 1865 and 1867 and served both to house soldiers and mount guns to protect the wharf. The armored brick enclosures in which the cannons were supposed to be placed were called casemates. However, by the time the brick casemates were complete, the guns were considered to be obsolete. In 1905, a three-story apartment building was constructed atop the fortified barracks, giving the barracks their present look. Over the years, the barracks have been home to soldiers, married officers and the Native American occupiers. When Alcatraz was a Federal Penitentiary, the barracks were known as building # 64. All newly arriving families to the island stayed in large but dismal apartments in building # 64 until an apartment in one of the three new buildings on the parade ground became vacant.

The fortified barracks (above, left) at ground level were built between 1865 and 1867, while the top three floors were added in 1905.

The dock tower (below, left and right) is the only free-standing guard tower remaining on Alcatraz.

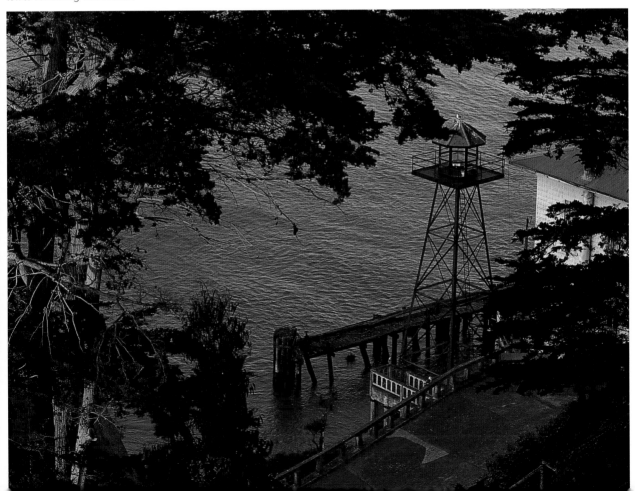

The guardhouse (opposite page), dates from 1857 and is the oldest standing building on Alcatraz.

The military chapel (above), built on top of the Sally Port in the 1920s, actually served several functions, including apartments and a school.

GUARDHOUSE AND SALLY PORT

The **guardhouse** served as one of the main defensive positions against enemies invading the island. Built in 1857, it is the oldest structure remaining on Alcatraz and is a vivid reminder of the days when it was the West Coast's most highly fortified military site. It could only be reached by an oak drawbridge that spanned a 15 foot deep dry moat. If attackers landed on the wharf and negotiated the dry moat, they would have encountered the **sally port**, a passage way with heavy, iron-studded wooden doors at each end and rifle slits lined the thick brick between the doors. Any attacker penetrating the first door would face a volley of gunfire from the military defenders. The sally port was never used to protect the island and during the Civil War the gunrooms were converted into prison cells. When the war ended and Alcatraz was designated a military prison, the sally port and guardhouse underwent further modifications in order to deal

with the influx of new prisoners. Those changes made in the 1870s completely enclosed the old guardhouse.

MILITARY CHAPEL

The last addition to the sally port and guardhouse was the two-story **military chapel** constructed on the roof of the building in the 1920s. The facade of the chapel was executed in the mission-revival style. The first floor contained living quarters for employees of the military prison and the second floor served as a school and occasionally a chapel. When Alcatraz became a Federal Penitentiary in 1934, the military chapel was converted into the bachelor quarters for unmarried correctional officers.

The burnt-out shell of the Officer's Club, destroyed by fire in 1970.

POST EXCHANGE

A short distance up the ascending road from the sally port sits the burnt-out skeleton of the **Post Exchange**, which was once the military PX (general store) before being converted to the Officers' Club during the years Alcatraz was a Federal Penitentiary. The Post Exchange was built in 1910 and it was the only place on the island where soldiers, officers and their families could buy food and other domestic items. As the social club for correctional officers and their families, The Post Exchange or Officer's Club, was the center of social activities of the island's small civilian community. It hosted dances, dinners, parties and other social events and contained a bowling alley and a gym. The building was gutted by fire in 1970, when several of the island's buildings burnt to the ground.

POWER PLANT

Not linked to the city's water and electricity supply, Alcatraz had to be self-sufficient. The **power plant** was built between 1910 and 1912 and the tall smokestack at the north end of the island has since been a landmark. The power plant was outfitted with generators that were powered by diesel fuel and supplied electricity to the entire island. The stories of some of the families that resided on Alcatraz during its years as a Federal Penitentiary mention the electrical supply not the cold wind or the isolation as the major inconvenience to life on the island. The diesel generator produced direct current, making most electrical appliances unusable. Converters that produced alternating current from the direct current were officially prohibited, since they overburdened the generators in the power plant. Despite that, many families managed to smuggle converters into their apartments.

The now inactive power plant was fired by diesel fuel and supplied the entire island with electricity (right).

NEW INDUSTRIES

The **New Industries Building** housed workshops and the laundry, which was the largest military laundry in the Bay Area and employed many inmates. In this building, along with the **Model Industries Building** below it, inmates manufactured a variety of articles, including gloves, furniture mats and army clothes. Today, the buildings and the adjacent areas are closed to visitors. The state of deterioration makes them a hazard and since they are not considered to be historically significant, there are no plans to restore them. They will either be demolished or left to crumble.

The New Industries Building also housed the laundry, which served Bay Area military bases and was the island's major industry. There are no plans to restore the building.

Water was always in short supply on Alcatraz until the Federal Bureau of Prisons built this 250,000 gallon water tower in 1939.

WATER TOWER

The lack of fresh water was an impediment to any human settlement on the island. When the U.S. Army began building fortifications on the island in 1852, engineers blasted cisterns in the sandstone to store captured rainwater and water was also carried to the island by boat. It seemed that no matter how many cisterns and water tanks the military installed, the supply of fresh water was always precarious. Since the prison industry on the island was a laundry, the Federal Bureau of Prisons built the 250,000 gallon steel water tank in 1939 and it remains one of the islands most visible landmarks.

The apartment buildings for officers and their families were torn down in 1971. Today, the ruins are slowly being covered by vegetation.

APARTMENTS/RUINS

Modern **living quarters** for the correctional officers and their families were built at the edge of the military parade grounds in the 1940s. Known as apartment buildings A, B, and C, most residents aspired to move there or into one of the cottages on the parade grounds. In 1971, following the end of the **Native American Occupation** of Alcatraz, the General Services Administration of the federal government demolished the apartment buildings as well as several other structures on the parade grounds in order to prevent them from being occupied illegally. Today, the debris from the concrete structures still is visible on the parade grounds. The **National Park Service** has opened the area to the public except certain times of the year when the seabirds are nesting.

The spacious warden's house (above, to the right of the lighthouse) was destroyed in June, 1970, when several fires broke out simultaneously on the island.

The present lighthouse was built in 1909, when the new cellhouse was under construction. The first lighthouse dated from 1854 (right).

WARDEN'S HOUSE

This once imposing house was reduced to a burnt-out shell on June 1 1970, when fires on several parts of the island were ignited simultaneously. Along with the **warden's house**, the fires also gutted the officer's club, the wooden prison doctor's house built in the 1880s and the living quarters of the lighthouse. The warden's house was built in 1926 when Alcatraz was a military prison and served as the residence of the U.S. Army Commandant. The home contained 18 rooms, most of them spacious, with tall windows providing spectacular views of the Bay and of San Francisco.

LIGHTHOUSE

In 1854, Alcatraz became home to the **first Pacific Coast Lighthouse** built by the United States. The first lighthouse, guided ships into the narrow entrance of San Francisco Bay and around the treacherous rocks of Alcatraz. Its light reflected from the oil lamps some 14 miles into the Pacific Ocean. The lighthouse keeper lit the lamps each evening, which he filled with sperm-whale oil. In 1909, when the new cellhouse was being built, the present 84-foot reinforced concrete lighthouse was constructed in order to be visible above the cellhouse. The oil lamps were replace by electric lamps, but keepers continued to run the lighthouse until 1963, when further changes were made and the lighthouse was automated. The beacon has shone every night from the middle of San Francisco Bay since 1854 except once, when fires destroyed the keeper's house on June 1, 1970. But the next evening, the lighthouse was powered by a generator supplied by the Native Americans who were occupying the island at the time.

CELLHOUSE

By the end of the 1800s it was apparent that the future of Alcatraz lay in its ability to hold men on the island rather than keeping enemies from invading it. As the island's prisoner population grew, the U.S. Army decided in 1907 to build a large, modern cellhouse atop the island. In the same year, Alcatraz was officially designated a military prison and the last defensive troops moved off the island.

The **cellhouse** was one of the features that enticed the federal government when it decided to take over Alcatraz in 1934. It was among the largest reinforced concrete structures in the world when it was completed in 1912. Ironically, much of the labor that went into constructing the cellhouse was contributed by the military inmates, meaning that these men were building their own prison. The new cellhouse rose on the foundations of the defensive barracks or citadel, which had been built in the 1860s. The famed dungeons where some of the Federal Penitentiary's prisoners were placed in solitary confinement in the 1930s were part of the old citadel.

The cellhouse was a prison within a prison. The four cellblocks, containing 600 cells, stood separately within the cellhouse without coming into contact with its walls or ceiling. The new cellhouse was also designed to be a self-contained prison with a dining room, kitchen, hospital, showers and library. Although it was a modern structure, whose features included electricity and steam heating, many modifications were made to increase security when Alcatraz became a Federal Penitentiary. The cellhouse never reached full capacity. The maximum number of inmates housed in the prison was 302, while there were 336 cells that had been remodeled for occupancy. The average number of prisoners on the island at any one time was 260.

Visitors today are inevitably drawn to the cellhouse, as it remains the most vivid symbol of the island's years as the country's most famous prison.

Completed in 1912, the cellhouse was built by the U.S. Army when the island's era as a defensive fort ended. Ironically, most of the labor to build the cellhouse was supplied by military convicts.

This vintage truck (above), parked next to the cellhouse, might have once carried supplies from the landing wharf to the prison.

The cellhouse on Alcatraz (below and right) was among the largest reinforced concrete structures in the world when it was completed in 1912.

The rocky shores of Alcatraz open up to magnificent views of San Francisco Bay (left).

Top: Alcatraz is once again an important nesting ground for seabirds, such as the Western gull.

FLORA AND FAUNA ON THE ISLAND

When Alcatraz was first sighted by Europeans, it truly deserved to be known as "The Rock." In comparison with the diverse and rich flora found on may parts of the island today, the barren sandstone rising out of San Francisco Bay originally supported very little vegetation. That started changing early in the island's inhabited history. While the army was building the fort on Alcatraz, it began hauling many thousands of tons of topsoil from nearby Angel Island. While native plants and grasses began sprouting from seeds contained in the soil, the residents of Alcatraz enjoyed planting gardens. This hobby became so popular that a gardening association was formed. Over time, more of the island became landscaped and terraced, particularly after fortifications were torn down when Alcatraz became solely a military prison. Since Alcatraz was abandoned in 1963, the gardens have overgrown their plots and vegetation has claimed more and more of the island. Today, the many plants and flowers that grow wild on Alcatraz constitute one of its most beautiful and interesting features.

Alcatraz was named after a **cormorant** not the pelican as popularly believed. Alcatraz was known by the early settlers of the area as **"Bird Island."** The lack of natural predators and the abundance of food from the Bay made the island a very hospitable breeding grounds for numerous species of sea birds. The bird population dwindled with the rise of human activity on the island, but today Alcatraz has once again become one of the most important habitats for birds in the Bay Area and even Northern California. The large Western Gull, is the most common bird on the island. Three species of cormorants and the black-crowned night herons also nest on the island, as do several species of land birds. Occasional visitors include the once nearly extinct brown pelicans and peregrine falcons.

Opposite page: Large gull colonies nest on Alcatraz, as do cormorants and the black-crowned night-herons. Brown pelicans are also occasional visitors.

Once a barren rock, Alcatraz has been radically transformed by human intervention. The planting of trees and gardens was made possible by importing tons of soil from nearby Angel Island. Today, the rich and varied flora seems to be slowly taking over much of Alcatraz and adds to the island's beauty.

Opposite page: Guard Station near watertower.

Entrance to Laundry area.

Seagulls on Pillar. (note bronze squirrel decoration)

ACTIVITIES ON ALCATRAZ AND SAN FRANCISCO BAY

Alcatraz Island is a prominent landmark in San Francisco Bay. It is well known to yachtsmen, recreational sailors, captains of container ships and merchant vessels which navigate the waters. The top left photo on page 94 depicts the start of the world famous "Escape from Alcatraz Triathlon." The race begins with a 1. 5 mile swim in 55° water from the shore off Alcatraz, to the beach near Fisherman's Wharf. The athletes proceed on a one mile run to the Marina Green and pick up their bicycles to ride 18 miles. The final portion of the triathlon is a treacherous run along the rugged coastline past the Golden Gate Bridge to Baker Beach. The Escape From Alcatraz is one of the most challenging triathlon courses in the world and attracts an international field of athletes.

Every year, in October, the Blue Angels fly in formation over San Francisco Bay to salute Fleet Week. The photo at the top of page 95 captures one of the Blue Angels flying upside down over Alcatraz. The Blue Angels use the Island as a key landmark for their precision maneuvers in formation over the Bay.

Opposite page, above: Beginning of the Escape from Alcatraz Triathlon.
Opposite page, below, and this page, middle: Sailing on San Francisco Bay.
This page, above: Blue Angels fly over Alcatraz.
This page, below: Large ships pass by Alcatraz enroute to the ports of Oakland and San Francisco.

CONTENTS